EVERYTHING YOU NEED TO KNOW ABOUT

LIVING IN A BLENDED FAMILY

GINA HAGLER

Rosen
YA™
New York

Published in 2019 by The Rosen Publishing Group, Inc.
29 East 21st Street, New York, NY 10010

Library of Congress Cataloging-in-Publication Data

Names: Hagler, Gina, author.
Title: Everything you need to know about living in a blended family / Gina Hagler.
Description: New York : Rosen Publishing Group, 2019. | Series: The need to know library | Audience: Grades 7–12. | Includes bibliographical references and index.
Identifiers: LCCN 2018005307| ISBN 9781508183495 (library bound) | ISBN 9781508183488 (pbk.)
Subjects: LCSH: Stepfamilies—Juvenile literature.
Classification: LCC HQ759.92 .H34 2019 | DDC 306.874/7—dc23
LC record available at https://lccn.loc.gov/2018005307

Manufactured in the United States of America

CONTENTS

INTRODUCTION

Families play an important role in societies around the globe. They exist for a variety of reasons, but among the most important is that they nurture the young. Children within a family receive the care and attention they require to grow and thrive. These days, there are many different kinds of families—some kids have one parent, some have two or more, and some kids acquire a new parent or two when their parents form new relationships. This could be the result of a breakup, divorce, or death, or when a single mother or father enters into a relationship. When adults in a family decide to form new relationships, these families are called blended families.

Blended families create units without biological ties. They create units comprising people who have no shared history. Everyone is involved in a process of change that affects each of them differently. Some blended families run smoothly from the start, but most have bumps at the start and along the way. The way those bumps are addressed and handled will make a difference in how well the new family performs as a unit.

It's often upsetting to have your parents break up and move on to new partners. It can be stressful to have new siblings, or to move to a new home. If all you've seen of blended families are movies about what used to be called stepfamilies, it's likely you have a lot of misinformation and confusion.

A family is made up of people who love and support each other, whether or not they are related by blood.

There are a number of common issues or problems that arise in blended families. You may not get along with your parent's new partner, and it can be hard to have to share your space with new siblings. You may be missing your other parent, and you may feel angry at one or both of your parents. You may be experiencing more serious problems, such as abuse or neglect.

If you're experiencing these issues, you may be feeling like you're the only one, but it's likely that thousands of people in blended families are going through the same things. It can be helpful to learn about some of the issues that arise in blended families so that you can be prepared to deal with them if they happen to you. The more you know about the potential bumps in the road, the better you are able to decide when and how to ask for help.

The changes that come about as a result of becoming a blended family are not all negative. You may find that this new family unit includes members you're happy to have in your life. It may lead to new opportunities and experiences. It may lead to a new normal that feels pretty good. It may also help you to see that change does not have to be bad. If it is handled well, it can be pretty good.

CHAPTER ONE

AM I THE ONLY ONE?

Y ou probably know you're not the only one who has ever had a parent divorce or die. You know you're not the only one with a parent who is remarrying. But knowing there are other people in the same position isn't the point. The point is that you find yourself in this position.

Still, there's something about understanding trends in relationships, marriage, divorce, and remarriage that goes a long way toward letting you know how normal your experience is. In the case of blended families, the trends show that you are definitely not alone. In fact, you have plenty of company.

FROM ONE PARENT TO TWO

According to the United States Census Bureau, 23 percent of children lived with a single mother in 2016. If you grow up living with a single parent, it's likely

When a couple decides to get married, they make a commitment to stay together for better or worse.

that your parent will date and may end up getting into a serious relationship with a partner. Whether or not they get married, you may come to think of this partner as your parent over time.

It can be hard to move from family to family, but it's not uncommon. In fact, according to Katherine Woodward Thomas, serial monogamy—that is, having a series of relationships over a lifetime, rather than one long-lasting relationship or marriage—is becoming the new norm. "Most of us will have several significant relationships in our lifetimes—not just one."

MARRIAGE AND DIVORCE

When two people marry, they make a promise to remain together for the rest of their lives. Yet, over the years, people and situations change. In decades past, societal pressure, social norms, and economic realities meant that married couples usually stayed together, even if they were unhappy. These days, if people are unhappy in a marriage, they are more likely to get divorced. In fact, according to the American Psychological Association, 40 to 50 percent of marriages end in divorce.

Most marriages that end in divorce do so in the first ten years. As a result, many people leave marriages with young children in tow. When parents are divorced, the children usually spend most of the time living with one parent and may visit their other parent every second weekend. Each family figures out the arrangement that works best for their situation.

NEW RELATIONSHIPS AND BLENDED FAMILIES

When single, separated, or divorced parents enter a new relationship and the relationship becomes serious, they may come together to form a new family unit. These families are known as blended families. Blended families are usually made up of two parents and the children from one or both of the parents' previous relationships.

Blended families are nothing new, yet they are usually not the families you see portrayed in the media. However, a closer look will tell you that many of the

Brad Pitt and Angelina Jolie's family was formed through adoption and the birth of children with biological ties to both parents.

celebrity families you see on TV are blended families, from Tom Brady of the New England Patriots and Gisele Bündchen, to Steven Spielberg and Kate Capshaw, to Brad Pitt and Angelina Jolie.

ALL RELATIONSHIPS REQUIRE WORK

Whatever the statistics show, the reality is that any relationship requires hard work and commitment. No relationship goes smoothly all the time. Every relationship—with friends, with siblings, and with parents—takes a sincere

FOSTER FAMILIES

Sometimes parents aren't able to take care of their own children for a variety of reasons, such as alcohol and substance abuse or if a parent is in jail. In this case, children and teens may go to live with a foster family. This may be a temporary situation while the parent gets his or her life back on track, or it may be for months or even years.

In a foster family, you will have to get used to living with your foster parents. There may be other foster kids in the family as well, and you will probably have to get used to going to a new school and making new friends, too. It's a big adjustment, and it's likely to be very emotionally stressful as well. You may be missing your parent and hoping to be reunited with her as soon as possible, or you may feel relieved to get away if you were being abused or neglected.

In an ideal situation, your foster parents will be kind and loving and will help you process your feelings and settle in. If this is not the case, or if you are being neglected or abused in your foster home, talk to your caseworker or another adult you trust about what is going on. There is no excuse for abuse or mistreatment in the foster care system or anywhere else.

effort on both sides. This is true for relationships within blended families as well.

There may be times when things are going well in your blended family, and times when they seem terrible. Being part of a new blended family means you are

Taking the time to get to know your stepparent can result in the development of a new relationship that you value.

involved in the creation of something new. You will have a role to play in the ups and downs that go with any new relationship. You will learn about yourself, how to communicate your feelings, and how to deal with new personalities as you work with your family members to create the blended family that works for you.

Some of the things that happen will be specific to your family. Others will be things that many other blended families have gone through. While not all blended families work out well, it may be helpful to know that many other kids have been through this process and come out with strong relationships with all of the adults in their lives.

MYTHS AND FACTS

MYTH: Adjusting to a blended family is quick and easy.

FACT: Any adjustment takes time and patience. Adjusting to a change in your living situation takes both because it touches on every aspect of your life. It's very stressful to learn to live with new people. Expecting the transition to be quick and easy will only make it harder. It's going to take time and effort on everyone's part to create a new family unit, so don't expect it to happen overnight.

MYTH: Blended families are not real families.

FACT: A "real" family is not defined by genetics. A "real" family is made up of people who love and respect one another. Its members look out for each other. They care when one family member is hurting or has a problem. Your commitment to one another, along with the bonds you create, is what makes a family a family.

MYTH: You will love your new parent as soon as you move in with her.

FACT: You are unlikely to instantly feel close to a new person in your life. In fact, you will probably have many emotions when your blended family is new. You and the other members of your family will need to work through these feelings. As you do, you will all grow to know and understand each other more deeply. These experiences will lead to deeper feelings for one another. If and when you feel respected and loved by your new parent, it is very likely you will grow to love this new parent. But this is not something you can rush. Remember to give it time and to be honest about your feelings so that you can work on your new relationship together.

CHAPTER TWO

HOW DOES THIS WORK?

Now that you are becoming part of a blended family, you may be wondering just how this is going to work. Will this new arrangement mean you'll be moving? Will you have new siblings? Are you changing schools? What about your other parent? What about your cousins and grandparents? How is this ever going to work?

IT'S NOT ALL NEW

You've probably had some time to get to know your parent's new partner. If your parent's new partner has children from a prior relationship, you've probably had some time to get to know them, too. Ideally, both parents have worked hard to answer your questions. Ideally, they'll also have anticipated some of your concerns and addressed them before they become issues. But things are not always ideal, of course.

If you're moving into someone else's house or apartment, this may seem a bit strange. You won't know

Getting used to a new blended family takes work. You may have to share your room with a new sibling. Sometimes it's not much fun.

where things are. It might not even feel like it's your home at first. If your stepparent and stepsiblings are moving in with you, it might feel strange to have other people roaming around your house, perhaps even sharing your bedroom. You'll need to make room for more people and their things. It's possible that some changes will be in store. These changes could be as simple as moving furniture around or as big as building a new room onto your house. The better you all communicate with each other about your needs and feelings, the better the process will go.

When your new mom knows what you like, she can make sure to add it to the list of things she buys at the grocery store.

While it's not *all* new, there is a lot that *is* new. If you stay in your house, you'll have new people in your home to adjust to. If you move to your parent's new partner's house, you will need to get used to living in a new place. Because of this, parents often choose to start blended family life in a house that is new to everyone. If this is the case, one of the first experiences you'll all share is the experience of your new home.

NEW HOUSE. NEW SCHOOL.

If you are going to be moving and starting a new school, chances are you're not delighted about it. Not only are you getting used to sharing your parent with a new person and new kids, but you are also getting used to a new house and a new school. It's a lot to deal with all at once.

One good strategy is to keep things as close to your usual routine as possible. If you always go to bed

FAMILY MEETINGS

A family meeting is a way to give everyone in the family a say in what's happening. At a family meeting, each family member gets a chance to bring up topics and ask questions. The adults may run the meeting and pick the topics, but there is usually a time for others to add their topics and concerns.

Some families have regular family meetings. They may take place after dinner on a certain night or at some other time. Other families have family meetings when the adults feel it is necessary. Still other families have family meetings whenever a member of the family requests one. Some families set an agenda—a list of the things to be discussed. Perhaps each family member picks a topic.

At a family meeting, a problem is discussed with input from everyone. It might be something like where to go for winter break. Each person can offer his or her suggestion. The family can brainstorm. You may not get your first choice, but you will have the opportunity to talk about your first choice as you all work together to reach a decision.

Family meetings are a great place to set the house rules: What are the bedtimes? Who is responsible for which chores? Which days can friends come over? What's the story on sleepovers? At the meeting, these topics can be decided with everyone's involvement.

One benefit of a family meeting is that it helps everyone learn to act as a team. It also gives everyone a chance to hear what the other family members have to say. You might find that someone else doesn't see a problem the same way you do. Once you know that, you can work to find a solution.

at a certain time, try to keep doing that. If you're used to doing your homework before dinner, stick with that schedule, too. If you lay out your clothes the night before, do that, even if it means laying them out in a different spot than you're used to. Be sure your favorite breakfast food is on the grocery list. Tell your new parent what you like for snacks. Speak up about the things that are important to you.

Sometimes a move means things change and you have to change with them. It may take longer to get to school, so you may have to get up earlier. Your homework load may be heavier than it was, so you may need to do homework before *and* after dinner. Your new siblings may play musical instruments and need to practice. Everyone may want their old friends over, and that may be too much at one time. While you're all working through these changes, it's easy to get frustrated. Taking turns to decide who gets their way each time you disagree can go a long way toward making this work. Try to keep in mind that it's an adjustment period and any adjustment takes a bit of getting used to.

THEY'RE STILL YOUR PARENTS

With all the excitement about your mom or dad's new partner, you may wonder what is going to change with your own parents. Your mom or dad is probably much happier than before. It may be odd to see your

It's not always easy to watch your mom being close to someone new. You may find yourself feeling jealous and left out.

parent holding hands with his or her new partner. They may even have a date night that doesn't include you at all.

And what about your other parent? If you have another parent that you're no longer living with, it's likely that you're missing him or her a lot. Perhaps your other parent is unhappy about your new blended family. Perhaps you feel uncomfortable moving between one parent and the other, especially if they ask you questions about what's going on in your new family or what you did when you were with your other parent. You may feel caught in the middle.

While it's certainly not easy, remember that this is all new for your parents as well, and it's probably not easy for them either. Ideally, they will work together to do what's best for you when things get complicated. They may have new people in their lives, but you are still their child. Try to be open with them so that they are aware when you're feeling confused or hurt, and hopefully they will work to make things easier on you.

CHAPTER THREE

THE CALM AFTER THE STORM

Y ou've made it through the adjustments. You've settled into your new routine. After all the worry and hurrying around and changes, it may be hard to believe this is real. The thing is, even when it's all good, it's still a family. All families have good times and bad times. While there are probably still things you miss from your old life, it's likely that some things are better than they were before.

YOUR PARENT IS HAPPIER

You may notice that your parent is a lot happier. He may be easier to talk to. He may be a lot more fun. You may not like sharing him, but maybe you can also see that sharing him isn't as hard as it used to be. It may even be fun to have a bigger family to do things with.

YOUR STEPPARENT IS REALLY TRYING HARD

You can see that your new stepparent is really trying. She remembers which foods you like and she's learned to cook a few of your favorite foods, too. She knows the names of your friends. She even knows the kind of toothpaste you like best. She's not your mom, but when you visit, you appreciate that she's ready to do things with you.

YOUR STEPPARENT IS ACTUALLY KIND OF COOL

Your stepparent is a great guy. He has taken the time to learn what you are good at and what you like. He asks about those things, and also invites you to do the things he likes. When he does, he makes those things fun, too. He and his kids make you feel included. He's not your dad, but he is a nice guy who is trying hard.

YOUR NEW FAMILY HAS A LOT OF FUN

Your parents used to fight all the time. Then, when they were angry, it was tense and nobody did anything together. Now your mom is happy and ready to go for hikes and on trips. You can tell that your new

It can be nice to have more family members to do activities with. Sometimes being part of a blended family can be fun.

siblings are happy with the new family, too. It may not always be fun to be in a blended family, but there are some benefits.

YOU ARE MAKING NEW TRADITIONS

The best part is that your dad and his new partner are planning to make this relationship permanent. You hope that will work, and sometimes you worry that it won't, but the fact that you're making new traditions is a good sign. It's also good because you have a say in the family traditions, like Sunday morning breakfasts and family movie nights.

IT'S NOT TOTALLY PERFECT

The one thing that worries you is that sometimes your dad and his new partner fight. Even though you know that people fight, it still makes you feel upset when they do because last time, all that fighting led to a divorce. Now here you are in a brand new family, and these adults are fighting.

Relationships are hard work. People argue. People disagree. It's not the fact that they disagree that is the problem. It's how they talk it through and decide on a way to settle the argument that matters. Think about your friends. If you never argue, is that because you agree about things all the time or because you don't like to argue. If you don't say what's bothering you, will it ever get fixed? Will you be able to stay friends in the long run?

Pay attention to the way your parent and her new partner argue. Pay attention to how they talk things through and resolve them. Chances are, they are working to find solutions that work. If you're still concerned, talk to your parent about it. You might even ask if you can call a family meeting to voice your concern.

IT'S NOT *THE BRADY BUNCH*

Maybe you've seen a TV show called *The Brady Bunch*. It was on the air in the 1970s, and it showed the day-to-day life in a blended family that was formed when a woman with three daughters married a man with three sons. There were lots of ups and downs as the boys and the girls learned to share their parent with three other kids.

(continued on the next page)

Don't worry if your blended family isn't like *The Brady Bunch*. That show didn't depict blended families in a very realistic way!

(continued from the previous page)

Everyone settled in and got used to the new family unit without too much craziness. Then, life went on with day-to-day arguments about homework, time in the bathroom, and who was better at everything from schoolwork to sports. Everyone got along. Everyone was mostly happy with the new blended family most of the time.

The Brady Bunch showed a blended family at its best. It was a family in which both adults were good listeners and caring parents and made time to deal with problems as they arose. All of the adults worked together to make the family work. When the children had a problem, an adult helped to work it through.

Even if your new family has made a great adjustment and is living happily together, it's probably not quite like *The Brady Bunch*. Don't worry. *The Brady Bunch* wasn't very realistic!

VISITING WITH YOUR OTHER PARENT

If you had two parents originally, you will probably have a system for visiting your other parent—the one you no longer live with—now that the separation or divorce is finalized. It will be strange at first, but once you get used to the routine, you may find that you enjoy these visits.

You may find that your parent is interested in doing new and different things. Perhaps he has started doing some things he enjoys during the time you aren't with him. You could ask to do those things with him. Maybe it will be photography or going to the movies. Maybe it will be hiking, or camping, or a cooking class. Whatever it is, it's a way for you to share time when you visit.

You may also go with your parent to visit your cousins and grandparents. This is a good chance for you to share the things you've been doing with them. You can bring some things from school that you're proud of. Maybe you'll bring along a new friend, too. Or, you can use these visits to stay connected to your old friends.

Being part of several family networks can be hard. You may have to spend some weekends in one home and others in a different one.

Maybe your parent is in a new relationship as well. You have some experience with this, so it may be easier for you to relax as you get to know his new partner. You know that being part of a blended family can be a positive thing.

REFLECTING ON YOUR EXPERIENCE

You might want to write about your experience of being part of a blended family. In your writing, you can reflect on the things that worked, the things that were challenging, and the ways your blended family handled these situations. There were probably some times when it seemed like a problem was too big to solve. How did your family handle those situations? Your experience of tackling these situations may well help you to cope with any tricky situations that arise later in your life.

CHAPTER FOUR

NOTHING IS THE SAME

S ometimes you get through the adjustment period and discover that things are simply not as good as you hoped. Maybe your new parent is demanding. Maybe your mom or dad is too busy to listen to you. Maybe it all just feels wrong. Knowing you're not the only kid in a blended family who feels this way may not be much help. You've still got to work your way through it each day.

MY NEW PARENT IS BOSSY

Maybe your dad's new partner is bossy. She doesn't listen. She says a child shouldn't argue with a parent. She says the rules for you are the same as the rules for her kids, but you think she treats them better than you. If you try to tell your dad about what she said, she interrupts or he says you need to work it out.

Part of the problem is that her kids already know her rules. They also know when she means business and when she's joking around. It's not easy for you to tell

Teachers and school counselors are there to help when a problem is too big for you to solve and your parents are not listening.

those things, and that makes you frustrated and sad. You really need your dad to help you out, and you're thinking of asking your mom to talk to your dad, but they are still fighting every time they see each other, so that probably won't work.

One thing you can do is wait until you are alone with your dad. Tell him you have something you need to speak to him about. If that doesn't work, it might be worth talking to a teacher you trust. Tell your teacher about the problem you're having and ask if she could speak to your dad with you.

IT'S NOT WHAT I THOUGHT IT WOULD BE

Many people learn about how blended families work from television shows and movies. In those media representations, things may be bumpy for a while, but they always work out in the end. In shows and movies, there's usually a bit of fun along the way. Right now, you may not be feeling like your family is very much fun. You may be feeling like nothing you thought you knew about blended families was accurate.

MY MOM LIKES MY NEW SISTER BETTER

You and your mom have always had a lot of fun together. Now you have a new sister who is nearly the

BLENDED FAMILIES IN THE MEDIA

There are several TV shows and movies that portray blended families. Each of these families is different from the others. Are any of these families like yours?

Drake & Josh: A TV show about two stepbrothers who are as different as it gets.

Modern Family: A TV show portraying several types of interconnected families, including traditional families, blended families, and same-sex parents.

The Fosters: A TV show about a lesbian couple and their multiracial blended family.

(continued on the next page)

This film still is from the 2005 remake of the 1968 movie *Yours, Mine, and Ours*, a comedy depicting a blended family made up of eighteen kids and two parents.

(continued from the previous page)

Full House: A TV show about three men—a widower, an uncle, and a best friend—who raise three kids together after their mother dies.

The Brady Bunch: A TV show about one widower and his three sons, one widow and her three daughters, and one housekeeper who loves them all.

Blended: A movie about one divorced mom, one widower dad, her kids, and his kids.

Yours, Mine, & Ours: A movie about one widower with ten kids, one widow with eight kids, plus a new baby.

same age as you. She and your mother laugh all the time. Your mom is always giving her a hug. Your sister is nice. It's just that your mom seems to like her better.

If you and your mom have always had a lot of fun together, it's doubtful that she likes this new sister better. She is probably trying to have a good relationship with her and doesn't notice that you are feeling left out.

Talk to your mom when you are alone with her. If you don't ever seem to be alone with her any more, tell her you really need to speak to her alone about something important. If that doesn't work, tell a teacher you trust about this problem. Ask if your teacher can have a meeting with you and your mom.

WE'RE HAVING A BABY

Your dad is over the moon. His new partner is having a baby. They told you this will be the first person in your family who doesn't have to adjust. That didn't sound good to you, but what could you say? Now you will have to adjust to living with a baby.

Babies are noisy. They need a lot of attention. They cry and make messes and need a lot of care. They may keep you awake at night, or make it hard for you to concentrate on your homework. They take your parents' attention away from you. You may even have to share a bedroom with this baby when it gets a bit older.

Fortunately, babies are also little bundles of curiosity and love. This new baby is going to have you as a sibling from the start. Chances are, you will develop a

A new baby can be fun. Then again, that new baby means another adjustment for your family.

close relationship with your baby sibling that will last a lifetime. While it seems like a lot of hassle now, it's likely you will grow to love and care about this new addition to the family.

MY PARENTS ARE FIGHTING OVER CUSTODY AND I'M STUCK IN THE MIDDLE

Sometimes, the hardest part of nothing being the same is the part that stays the same. Even though he hardly

WHAT ABOUT ME?

In the old days, it was your parents and you. They fought. Things got ugly. Most of the time it was no fun, but at least you knew how things worked. Perhaps you have siblings, cousins, aunts and uncles, and grandparents, too. All of this may have formed a system that worked well enough, even if it wasn't perfect. Now there are new players. There's a new parent and, perhaps, new siblings, cousins, aunts and uncles, and grandparents. Maybe you're not sure where you fit in.

It's perfectly normal to feel anxious as everyone settles in to a new normal. Some anxiety may be the type you feel before any big event. Some may be caused by the changes taking place. Some may be because everyone around you is anxious. Talk to your parent. Let him or her know you need a bit of support as all of you create a blended family.

ever sees her, your dad is still saying nasty things about your mom. It might be about what she fed you when you visited her. It might be the way she put your clothes in your backpack. Sometimes it feels like it doesn't matter—the fighting is never going to stop.

One of the hardest things for kids is when parents can't come to an amicable agreement about sharing custody, so they have an ugly battle in court over it. Perhaps your parents are putting pressure on you to pick a side. This is an unfair situation to put a child or teen in. If you are feeling overwhelmed and you don't feel you can talk to either of your parents about it, try talking to a teacher, a school counselor, or another adult you trust.

You shouldn't have to feel guilty because you love both your parents. You have a special relationship with each of your parents that is separate from their relationship with each other. You may not like the way they treat each other, but you are entitled to have a loving relationship with each of them.

I DIDN'T ASK FOR A DAD

If you grew up with a single parent, you may be wishing things had stayed the same. You were perfectly happy with one parent, and you never asked for a dad. This can be a particularly hard situation to deal with because many people believe that kids need two parents. Maybe your mom feels that she did the right thing for you by marrying or moving in with her partner, because now your family has a bigger apartment or more money.

Meanwhile, you may be feeling that you didn't ask for those things, and you were happier when it was just you and your mom and you got to spend more quality time together. Maybe you will learn to love your new dad eventually, or maybe you won't. Either way, you are entitled to your feelings. If you can't talk to your mom about how you're feeling, find a friend you can talk openly with.

CHAPTER FIVE

THIS IS NOT WORKING

S ometimes, even after a transition period, things may still not be working. You may worry that it's your fault, but it is the job of the adults to work things out.

YOU'RE THE ONLY ONE MAKING AN EFFORT

You're doing what you can to make the family work. You're sharing your things, caring about your new family members, spending time with the new people in your extended family, and trying to have a positive outlook. But there's nothing you can do if the other kids are not doing their part. Cleaning up their messes, lying for them, speaking up for them—none of that is your role. Your role is to speak to your parent about how the behavior of the other kids is a problem, then let the adults take care of it. If your parent isn't helping, talk to a teacher or school counselor.

YOU WISH YOU COULD LIVE WITH YOUR OTHER PARENT

You may be missing your other parent even more than usual when things are not working out with your new family. It is upsetting to find yourself in a new home with new people but the same old problems are there. There's fighting with no solution. It's frightening, and you wish you could be with your other parent, where things would probably be calmer.

Perhaps your other parent lives too far away for you to live with him, or perhaps your parents have decided where you have to live and you have no say in the matter.

It is stressful and upsetting to hear your parents arguing. If the fighting gets too bad or you feel unsafe, reach out for help.

Chances are, the parent you live with is not going to be happy to hear that you'd rather live with your other parent. But that doesn't mean you can't have those feelings. Try to find someone you can talk to, such as a school counselor or teacher. Maybe they can work with your family to find a way for you to spend more time with your other parent or help to make things work a bit better in your new blended family. Even if they can't help you change your living situation, they may be able to listen and help you process your feelings. Sometimes just talking openly about how you feel can help you to feel better.

THE FIGHTING IS WORSE

This is every kid's nightmare scenario. You go through all the steps necessary to form a blended family, but then the fighting is worse than ever. Think about whether it really is worse, or if it just feels worse because you hoped there wouldn't be any fighting at all. This is certainly not a problem you can tackle on your own. You will need to go to a school counselor to see what help she can give you in addressing this with your parent and his new partner.

YOUR NEW PARENT ISN'T PAYING ATTENTION TO YOU

Being busy is one thing. Neglecting a member of your family is another thing altogether. It may be that your stepparent is a quiet person who doesn't interact very

Everyone feels lonely sometimes, but if you find yourself feeling lonely and neglected a lot of the time, it's time to speak to an adult you trust, such as a teacher or a school counselor.

much with anyone. If that's the case, you'll need to learn to have a relationship that may not be the one you'd hoped for.

However, if your new parent has time and attention for everyone but you, that's not OK. It isn't your responsibility to try to please someone who doesn't seem interested in having a relationship with you. If you're being neglected or ignored within your own family, you should speak to another family member or a teacher or school counselor and let them know how this behavior is affecting you.

WHERE TO GO FOR HELP

If you're being abused by a family member and you don't know where to turn for support, there are a number of organizations that can provide you with confidential assistance and refer you to local service providers in your area.

RAINN National Sexual Assault Telephone Hotline
Call 800-656-HOPE (4673) to be connected with a sexual assault service provider in your area. Calls are confidential and are answered twenty-four hours a day. Find out more at www.RAINN.org.

Childhelp National Child Abuse Hotline
Call 1-800-4-A-CHILD (422-4453) to connect with crisis counselors and get confidential information and referrals. Staff members speak over 177 languages and answer calls twenty-four hours a day. Find out more at www.ChildHelp.org/hotline.

The National Domestic Violence Hotline
Call 1-800-799-7233 or 1-800-787-3224 (TTY) for confidential assistance and referrals to service providers in your area. Find out more at www.TheHotline.org.

YOUR NEW PARENT IS ABUSING YOU

There is no circumstance ever that makes it OK for an adult to mistreat you emotionally, verbally,

It is never OK for an adult to lose control when speaking to or disciplining you. If there is abuse happening in your family, there are advocates who can help.

physically, or sexually. It doesn't matter if the adult had a bad day. It doesn't matter if the adult has a bad temper and needs to let off steam. It doesn't matter if your new parent isn't good with words. This behavior is unacceptable.

Emotional abuse means that your parent is loving and caring one day, then screaming and hypercritical the next. It means that you never know what to expect when you need the emotional support of that parent or other family member.

Verbal abuse means that your new parent is calling you mean names and making you feel uncomfortable about yourself. You may not like nicknames and you may find it irritating when someone uses one with you, but being abused is not about well-meaning but annoying nicknames. It's about an adult deliberately using words to make you feel terrible about yourself.

Physical abuse means that your new parent is hitting you or punishing you severely. It doesn't matter what you did—an adult should be able to deal with you without losing control. If you are being physically harmed by your parent or her partner, go to your teacher immediately and tell her. She should then follow the necessary steps to investigate and to ensure that you are safe.

Telling a teacher or another adult about any kind of abuse is not snitching. It is not creating a problem. It is how you protect yourself from inappropriate behavior on the part of an adult.

Sexual abuse means that your new parent is touching you inappropriately, watching you when you are doing private activities, or asking you to do physical things that are far outside the scope of what an adult should ask. If a person ever touches you, or asks you to touch him or her, and then tells you not to tell anyone—that it's a secret between the two of you—that is a sign that it's abuse. This is a crime.

Tell your parent immediately. If he or she does nothing—or worse yet, says it is your fault—go to a teacher or school counselor as soon as you can. You may worry that this will make things worse, but you are not making things worse. You are dealing with a very difficult situation in a mature way.

IT'S NOT YOUR FAULT

It's easy to blame yourself if things aren't working out in your family—to imagine things would be better if you changed your behavior or did something differently. The truth is, there is very little one person can do to make a whole family work if the other family members aren't trying. You need to do your part, but you can't do everything.

CHAPTER SIX

A NEW NORMAL

In movies and on television, problems between friends and family members are usually worked through and solved by the time the show ends. In real life, there is rarely a neat, happy ending—especially when a problem is complicated or involves several people.

GIVE IT TIME

You and the members of your blended family are creating something new. Creating anything new takes ongoing effort such as writing a paper, creating a work of art, or building a computer from parts. There will be times when things work on the first try. There will be times when it takes several tries and maybe even some extra help. And there will be times when it just doesn't work at all.

The same is true with your blended family. It may be months or even years before you feel like your

Doing fun things together, like bowling, can strengthen relationships within your new family.

family is your real family. You and your new siblings may form a close bond as soon as you move in together, or it could take years. You may feel competitive and jealous of each other. Try to remember that your new siblings are also adjusting to a new reality.

Remember that a blended family is not just about one relationship but about a network of relationships. Each person has a stake in the relationships in the family. Even if your part is running smoothly, the other parts may not be. Because of this, one of the best things you can do is to view the creation of a blended family as a work in progress. Don't expect it to be perfect from the start. Don't take every bump in the road as a sign that it is not working. Remember the times you've learned something new or tackled a new skill. Give your new family the same patience you gave those things.

YOU CAN'T DO IT ALONE

Relationships take work. A blended family is a network of relationships. Each family member needs to work on making these relationships work. This means paying attention to how everyone is feeling, addressing any problems that arise, and working toward solutions that meet the needs of the entire family.

Kids and adults alike value stability. Everyone needs a place that's relatively free from conflict and drama.

(continued on the next page)

It's important for each person to be heard and valued in any family. Some families address this by having family meetings, where all family members have a chance to discuss any issues they have.

(continued from the previous page)

Everyone wants a place at the table, literally and figuratively. That certainly can happen in a blended family, but it's not something that one person can make happen—especially a child.

You may be feeling like it's your responsibility to make sure everything works out in your family. You may think that you have the answer or know just what to do. You certainly need to do your part, but you can't do it all on your own.

In the end it is up to the adults to have a vision and a plan for this new family. It's up to them to take the lead and help everyone to work together. The adults are the ones who must sort through the complications that are part of combining two households. It is up to them to make each kid feel heard, valued, and cared about.

THERE'S NO SUCH THING AS A REAL MOM OR DAD

It can be difficult when someone outside your family asks about your "real" parents. They probably mean the parent who is your biological or birth parent, but that doesn't always help. When someone asks about your "real" parent, that implies that your other parent is somehow not real. It makes it sound like the only relationships that matter are with your biological parents.

You are in a position to know that there is no such thing as a real parent. In your blended family, there are adults who care for you on a day-to-day basis, as well as adults who may only see you once or twice a week. All of these adults are parents to you. All of these adults are people who have a loving interest in your well-being.

The adults who parent you are your real parents, whether there are one, two, three, or four of them and whether they are two moms, two dads, a mom and a dad, or any other combination. The family you live in is a real family, whether or not it is a blended family. Just as you are not a fake person, your parents and family are not fake. It's all as real as it gets. Being confident of this is part of what it takes to make it work.

ACKNOWLEDGE YOUR FEELINGS

Your childhood is the foundation for the rest of your life. Forming a new family can be disruptive and emotionally difficult, but it can also make you stronger.

You may sometimes feel sad that your parents are divorced or that one of them has passed away. Those are normal feelings and it's OK—and good—to talk about them. It is also OK to be happy when things are going well in your new family. There is no need to feel torn between being happy in your new family and being loyal to something that no longer exists. Talk to your parents if you are feeling confused or

If one of your parents lives far away, you may only be able to communicate with him or her via Skype or FaceTime. It's normal to feel sad about this, and it's always good to talk about your feelings.

conflicted about your feelings. The adults in your life want you to be happy, and they can help you process your feelings. If you can't talk to your parents or you need more help, seek out a trusted teacher or a school counselor to talk to.

The bottom line is, your blended family is now your family. Just as in any family, there are probably still things that make you sad, but you may also find that you are happy and that you enjoy aspects of being in this new family. Be sure to acknowledge and celebrate those happy feelings, too.

10 GOOD QUESTIONS TO ASK A SOCIAL WORKER

1. My dad's new partner wants me to call her Mom. I already have a mom. I don't want to hurt her feelings or make her angry. What should I do?
2. We're having a new baby. Everyone else is excited but I'm not. Is there something wrong with me?
3. It used to be just me and my sister. Now we have a new sister. She and my sister spend all their time together. What about me?
4. Can I be part of two families at once? How is that possible?
5. My new parent tells me what to do. He says I have to listen to him, but he's not my dad. Do I have to listen to him?
6. My mom has a new boyfriend almost every year. We're always moving from place to place. She says I have to call them Dad, but I don't feel like they're my dad. What should I do?
7. What if my dad also marries someone new? I don't like the idea of other kids living with my dad. I don't like feeling so angry and sad. What can I do?

8. I can only bring two parents to my school con-cert. I wasn't going to tell my dad, but his new partner found out. She's all excited to see me play. If they both come then my mom can't come. Who should I bring?

9. I can see that my new brother is not happy to share his grandpa with me. I never had a grandpa, so it would be fun to have one, but I understand how he feels. What should I do?

10. I think my new family is fun, but I still feel bad that my parents are not together. I should be happier. Is there something wrong with me?

adoption The legal process of becoming a child's official parent.

birth parents The people whose DNA create a person.

blended family The family that is formed when two adults enter a relationship and bring their children (possibly from prior relationships) together to form a new family unit.

counselor A person who is licensed and trained to help people with the issues in their lives.

divorce The legal end of a marriage.

family therapy A type of therapy for families to work through their issues together.

foster care A temporary placement of a child with a family who cares for that child without assuming parental rights.

genetics The traits that people inherit from their birth parents.

interrelate When two or more parts interact with each other.

network A system in which many parts or people interrelate.

reflect To think carefully about something.

relationship The interactions that occur between two people or things; within a family, each person has a relationship with each other person in the family.

remarry To marry again after a divorce or the death of a spouse.

sibling A brother or sister with the same parent or parents.

speculation An educated guess.

stepfamily An older term used for a blended family.

therapy The process of talking through issues with a trained counselor.

thrive To do especially well in a given situation.

tradition A meaningful custom that is handed down from one generation to the next.

trauma A very bad injury or an experience that causes psychological injury or pain.

vow A personal commitment or serious promise.

widow A woman whose spouse has died.

widower A man whose spouse has died.

American Psychological Association (APA)
750 First Street, NE
Washington, DC 20002
(800) 374-2721; (202) 336-5500; TDD/TTY (202)336-6123
Website: http://www.apa.org
Facebook: @AmericanPsychologicalAssociation
The APA has more than 115,700 researchers, educators, and clinicians working to promote psychological health in individuals and families. Its Psychology Help Center has material for blended families.

Canadian Stepfamily Institute
British Columbia
Canada
(250) 619-9555
Website: http://thecanadianstepfamilyinstitute.ca
Facebook: @DianneMartinStepfamilyCounsellor
The Canadian Stepfamily Institute provides workshops and support for step- and blended families. It received the Foundations of Cybercounselling Award from the University of Toronto.

Hand in Hand Parenting
555 Waverley Street, Room 25
Palo Alto, CA 94301
(219) 854-7900
Website: https://www.handinhandparenting.org
Facebook: @handinhandparenting

Hand in Hand Parenting is a nonprofit that works with parents of young children to provide research, training, and support.

National Stepfamily Resource Center
Center for Children, Youth, and Families (CCYF)
Auburn University
Auburn, AL 36849
(334) 844-3790
Website: http://www.stepfamilies.info
The National Stepfamily Resource Center is a division of the Auburn University CCYR. Its mission is to serve as a clearinghouse of information that links family science research on blended families and best practices in work with couples and children in stepfamilies.

Parent Encouragement Program (PEP)
10100 Connecticut Avenue
Kensington, MD 20895
(301) 929-8824
Website: http://pepparent.org
Facebook: @pepparent
PEP provides classes and educational resources for parents and childcare providers. The PEP mission is to build strong families through education, skill building, and support.

Step and Blended Family Institute
12 Metcalf Crescent
Tottenham, ON L0G 1W0

Canada
(905) 936-7837
Website: http://www.stepinstitute.ca/what_we_do.php
The Step and Blended Family Institute provides
    services ranging from resources to coaching to
    therapy, with a mission of helping step- and blended
    families thrive.

Stepfamily Foundation
Jeannette Lofas, LCSW
310 West 85th Street, Suite 1B
New York, NY 10024
(212) 877-3244
Website: http://www.stepfamily.org
Facebook: @stepfamily
The Stepfamily Foundation provides counseling, semi-
    nars, and other services for families during divorce,
    remarriage, and the creation and maintenance of a
    step/blended family.

FOR FURTHER READING

Blume, Judy. *It's Not the End of the World*. New York, NY: Atheneum Books for Young Readers, 1972.

Buxbaum, Julie. *Tell Me Three Things*. New York, NY: Delacorte Press, 2016.

Gagnon, Michelle. *Unearthly Things.* New York, NY: Soho Teen, 2017.

Johansson, J R. *Cut Me Free.* New York, NY: Farrar, Straus & Giroux, 2015.

Kavanaugh, Dorothy. *Hassled Girl? Girls Dealing with Feelings.* Berkeley Heights, NJ: Enslow Publishers, 2014.

Mac, Carrie. *10 Things I Can See from Here.* New York, NY: Alfred A. Knopf, 2017.

Maskame, Estelle. *Did I Mention I Love You?* Naperville, IL: Sourcebooks Fire, 2015.

Maskame, Estelle. *Did I Mention I Miss You?* Naperville, IL: Sourcebooks Fire, 2016.

Nadin, Joanna, and Eglantine Ceulemans. *The Stepmonster.* London, UK: Egmont UK Limited, 2016.

Nielsen-Fernlund, Susin. *We Are All Made of Molecules.* New York, NY: Ember, 2016.

Rosinsky, Lisa. *Inevitable and Only*. Honesdale, PA: Boyds Mills Press, 2017.

Tolan, Stephanie S, and R J. Tolan. *Applewhites Coast to Coast.* New York, NY: Harper, 2017.

American Psychological Association. "Marriage and Divorce." Retrieved March 3, 2018. http://www .apa.org/topics/divorce.

Baer, Drake. "Remarriage Is the New American Marriage." Cut, 2017. https://www.thecut.com /2017/02/how-many-people-in-america-get -remarried.html.

Banschick, Mark. "The High Failure Rate of Second and Third Marriages." Psychology Today, 2012. https://www.psychologytoday.com/blog/the -intelligent-divorce/201202/the-high-failure-rate -second-and-third-marriages.

Bray, James. "Making Stepfamilies Work." American Psychiatric Association, 2018. http://www.apa.org /helpcenter/stepfamily.aspx.

Centers for Disease Control and Prevention. "Marriage and Divorce." National Center for Health Statistics, March 17, 2017. https://www.cdc.gov/nchs /fastats/marriage-divorce.htm.

Centers for Disease Control and Prevention. "National Marriage and Divorce Rates." Retrieved February 15, 2018. https://www.cdc.gov/nchs/data/dvs /national_marriage_divorce_rates_00-16.pdf.

Chapman, Kate. "The Ugly Truth About Blended Families." HuffPost, February 2, 2017. https:// www.huffingtonpost.com/entry/the-ugly-truth -about-blended-families_us_589363b6e4b0b4 d609210569.

Coontz, Stephanie. *Marriage, a History: How Love Conquered Marriage.* New York, NY: Penguin Books, 2006.

Coontz, Stephanie. *The Way We Never Were: American Families and the Nostalgia Trap.* New York, NY: Basic Books, 2016.

Coontz, Stephanie. *The Way We Really Are: Coming to Terms with America's Changing Families.* New York, NY: Basic Books, 1997.

GoodTherapy.org. "Communication Problems." January 3, 2017. https://www.goodtherapy.org /learn-about-therapy/issues/communication-issues.

KidsHealth.org. "Foster Families." Retrieved March 26, 2018. https://kidshealth.org/en/kids/foster -families.html.

Manning, Wendy D. "Cohabitation and Child Wellbeing." US National Library of Medicine, from Future Child, Fall 2015. https://www.ncbi.nlm.nih .gov/pmc/articles/PMC4768758.

Reeves, Richard V., and Eleanor Krause. "Cohabiting Parents Differ from Married Ones in Three Big Ways." Brookings, April 15, 2017. https://www .brookings.edu/research/cohabiting-parents -differ-from-married-ones-in-three-big-ways.

Swanson, Ana. "144 Years of Marriage and Divorce in the United States, in One Chart." *Washington Post*, June 23, 2015. https://www.washingtonpost .com/news/wonk/wp/2015/06/23/144-years-of -marriage-and-divorce-in-the-united-states-in-one -chart/?utm_term=.a46bf8f5d064.

Thomas, Katharine Woodward. "Why Serial Monoga-my Is the New Marriage." *Glamour*, May 21, 2015. https://www.glamour.com/story/serial-monogamy -marriage-conscious-uncoupling.

Wallerstein, Judith S. "Nine Psychological Tasks for a Good Marriage." American Psychiatric Associa-tion. Retrieved February 27, 2018. http://www.apa .org/helpcenter/marriage.aspx.

Wevorce. "Why Do Second Marriages Fail?" January 9, 2017. https://www.wevorce.com/blog/why -do-second-marriages-fail.

ABOUT THE AUTHOR

Gina Hagler is an author and educator who works with students in grades K–12. She is an adoptive mom who is part of a blended family. She has had an active interest in marriage, divorce, and blended families for many years. As a result, she has read widely on the subject and spoken to many professionals involved in activities that support healthy blended families.

PHOTO CREDITS